CONTENTS

WHAT IS SUSTAINABLE FOOD?

Sustainable food causes as little harm to the environment as possible. It is grown without making it more difficult to grow food in the future.

Here is just one example of non-sustainable versus sustainable food (there are lots of others later in this book):

CASE 1

A farmer adds lots of chemicals to the soil to make the plants grow better. The trouble is, the chemicals also drain the soil of nutrients. Next year, the farmer will have to add more chemicals. Eventually, even with chemicals added it will be difficult to grow food on the soil.

THIS IS NOT SUSTAINABLE!

CASE 2

The farmer decides not to use chemicals. Instead, the fields are used to grow several different crops. Each crop needs slightly different nutrients, so the soil is not drained. The farmer grows slightly less than with chemicals. But the soil stays just as good for growing crops.

THIS IS SUSTAINABLE!

Crops being sprayed with insect-killing chemicals.

WHY DO WE NEED SUSTAINABLE FOOD?

One big reason we need sustainable food is that the world's population is increasing every year:

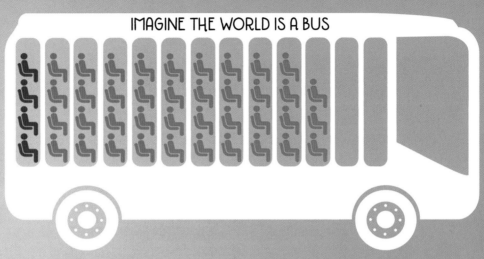

IMAGINE THE WORLD IS A BUS

In 1900, there were **1.6 billion** passengers.

By 2000, there were **6 billion** passengers.

In 2050, experts think there will be **9.5 billion** passengers.

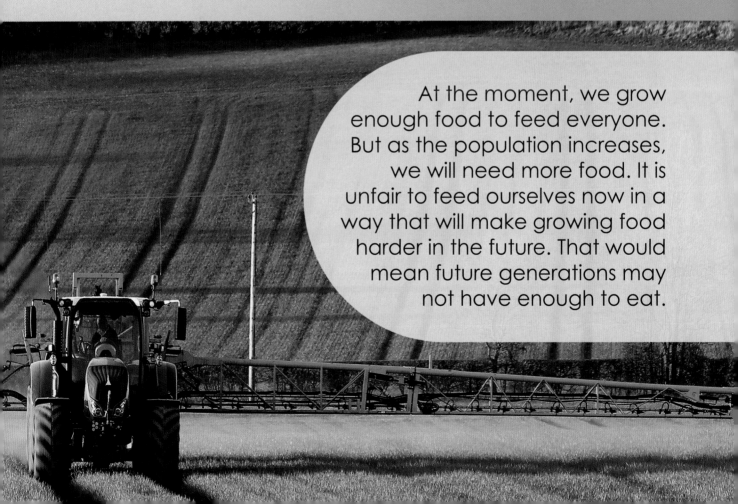

At the moment, we grow enough food to feed everyone. But as the population increases, we will need more food. It is unfair to feed ourselves now in a way that will make growing food harder in the future. That would mean future generations may not have enough to eat.

FAIR TRADE

Farmers are not always able to get a fair price for the food they grow. The idea of 'fair trade' is that farmers should always be paid enough to make a profit.

WHY IS FAIR TRADE IMPORTANT?

First, because if farmers do not earn enough money, they will have to close their farms. Then there will be no one left to grow our food. This is obviously not sustainable!

Second, if farmers do not earn enough, they may be forced to make unsustainable choices. They might decide to use extra chemicals on the soil, for example. These chemicals will produce a bigger crop in the short term, but may harm the environment in the future.

THE CHANGING VALUE OF MILK

In the UK, between 2010 and 2015, the amount farmers were paid per litre of milk went up, then down again. By 2015, some farmers were not making any money from selling milk.

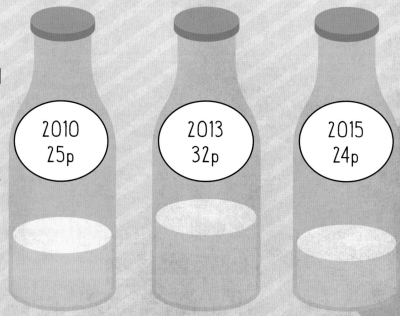

2010
25p

2013
32p

2015
24p

Most of us drink milk or eat milk-based food, such as cheese, so we need to make sure dairy farmers can keep providing milk in the future.

THE MOO MAN

The Moo Man is a film about a dairy farmer who lives near Hailsham, in England. His name is Steve Hook.

A few years ago, Steve's farm was in danger of going out of business. He was selling his milk to supermarkets for 27p a litre. The trouble was, it cost more than that to produce. Every litre of milk sold actually cost Steve money!

Steve stopped selling milk to supermarkets. Instead, he started delivering it straight to his customers. Some were local people who became part of a milk round. Others – as far away as Scotland! – had their milk delivered by courier. Steve also sold milk at local markets. Selling direct meant he could get a higher price than by selling it to the supermarkets.

WHERE IS YOUR FOOD FROM?

Food that comes from far away is usually less sustainable than food from nearby.

Trucks, boats, planes and trains are all used to transport food. They all release a gas called carbon dioxide, or CO_2. This gas is one of the causes of global warming. Global warming is causing desertification around the world. Because of desertification, every year there is less land for growing food. This is not sustainable.

If your food is only transported a short distance before you buy it, less CO_2 is released. So one feature of sustainable food is that it is not transported long distances. Instead, it is grown as near as possible to where it will be eaten.

WHERE IS YOUR LETTUCE FROM?

Driving lettuces from Morocco to London releases about **342 kg** of **CO_2**

Driving lettuces from Spain to London releases about **185 kg** of **CO_2**

Driving lettuces from Canterbury to London releases about **10.7 kg** of **CO_2**

A lettuce driven to market from a farm far away causes more pollution than a lettuce from nearby.*
*these figures are based on truck journeys.

The Greenmarket Farmers' Market in Union Square, New York, is open for four days a week.

GREENMARKET FARMERS' MARKETS

Greenmarket Farmers' Markets started in Union Square, Manhattan, USA in 1976. A few farmers from close to the city set up a market. It was a way for them to sell their crops directly to shoppers. It also gave New Yorkers a chance to buy fresh, locally grown food.

The idea of a farmers' market became so popular that today there are more than 50 similar markets in the area. Everything has to be grown in the region, rather than being transported a long distance. (All the food also has to be grown or made by the people selling it.) This means transporting the food to market has a small environmental impact.

HOW DOES YOUR FOOD REACH YOU?

Imagine your next meal being flown to your house in a helicopter. Sounds fun! But helicopters release lots of pollution. This is not good, if you want sustainable food.

Now imagine your next meal arriving at your house by bicycle. Bikes cause ZERO pollution. In the sustainable-food game, the meal that arrives by bike is the winner.

TYPICAL FOOD TRANSPORT

Of course, food is not usually delivered by helicopter or bike. So how does it travel?

- Small trucks bring all kinds of food short distances
- Big trucks transport food thousands of kilometres
- Boats are used for longer distances, especially for food that does not need to stay fresh
- Airplanes carry fresh food long distances

Transporting food by air produces a LOT of pollution.

POLLUTION FROM FOOD TRANSPORT

0.733 kg of **CO_2 per km**
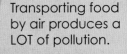

0.303 kg of **CO_2 per km**

0.107 kg of **CO_2 per km**

A Barcombe vegetable delivery box, ready to be left on a customer's doorstep.

FOOD-BOX DELIVERY SCHEME

Every week in Barcombe, England, boxes of fresh food are packed for delivery. Most of the food is grown by Barcombe Nurseries. Almost everything else is grown by other farmers very close by. A tiny amount comes from further away.

Once a selection of food has been packed into boxes, Barcombe's van sets out on its delivery round. Each box is delivered to the customer's door. Instead of hundreds of people making trips to the supermarket to buy food, just one van drives around delivering a whole week's fresh supplies.

Food-box delivery schemes like this are a great way of making food more sustainable.

GROWING FOOD

Before your food even starts its journey to your table, it has already caused a lot of pollution. In fact, growing food often produces MORE pollution than transporting it.

83 per cent of _____ emissions come from growing food

17 per cent come _____ from everything else (storage, transport, etc.)

HOW CAN GROWING FOOD CAUSE SO MANY EMISSIONS?

To understand this, think about tomatoes.

If you like tomatoes, you probably like eating them all year. But in northern Europe and North America, tomatoes don't grow all through the year. You have two choices:

Choice 1
Buy tomatoes that have been flown or driven from somewhere hot.

Choice 2
Buy tomatoes grown nearby in a heated greenhouse.

Imagine you are a Swedish tomato lover. Which is the best choice?

LONG-HAUL VERSUS GREENHOUSE TOMATOES

From what you learned on pages 8–11, you would probably guess that the greenhouse tomatoes grown nearby are best. But you would be wrong:

FROM SWEDEN

FROM SPAIN

Transport: 300 g
Production: 230 g
Fertilisers: 200 g

Transport: 68 g
Production: 3,800 g
Fertilisers: 47 g

Units: g CO_2 per kg of tomatoes

The tomatoes from Spain cause far fewer total emissions – even though their transport emissions are more than four times as high. This is because keeping a Swedish greenhouse warm enough to grow tomatoes uses a lot of energy.

Most of our energy comes from burning fossil fuels. Doing this releases CO_2 into the air. When you add these CO_2 emissions into the tomato total, it has a big effect.

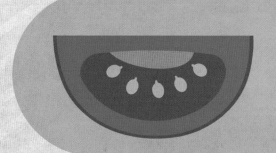

SEASONAL FOOD

Experts agree that eating local, seasonal food is a good way to eat sustainably. But what IS seasonal food?

Most foods grow at a particular time of year. For example, in England, raspberries grow in summer and autumn. In southern Australia, kiwi fruit grows in winter.

Each food has a season when it naturally grows. Eating it during that season means you are eating seasonal food.

OUT-OF-SEASON CHOICES

Imagine you want raspberries at Christmas. They do not naturally grow in the UK at Christmas. If you want to buy local raspberries, they have to be grown in a heated greenhouse. The infographic on page 13 shows how unsustainable that would be!

The other choice would be to have raspberries that have been flown to you from somewhere hot. The infographic on page 10 shows what an unsustainable idea that is!

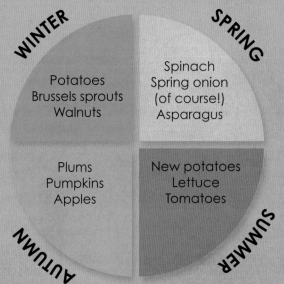

WINTER
Potatoes
Brussels sprouts
Walnuts

SPRING
Spinach
Spring onion
(of course!)
Asparagus

AUTUMN
Plums
Pumpkins
Apples

SUMMER
New potatoes
Lettuce
Tomatoes

Seasonal foods are different depending on where you live. These are common ones in temperate climates.

An Ethicurean chef picks part of tonight's menu.

THE ETHICUREAN

Near the English city of Bristol is a restaurant called The Ethicurean. Its mission is to show that seasonal food is more sustainable and more interesting than eating the same things all year.

The restaurant is next door to a walled garden, where a lot of its food is grown. This food really does not travel far before being eaten! The meat is either from local farms or hunted in the wild nearby.

Because what is growing outside changes all the time, the restaurant's menu also changes through the year.

PROTECTING THE SOIL

To be able to grow food in the future, we will need fertile farmland. However, today's farming methods sometimes harm the land.

INTENSIVE FARMING

Intensive farming is a way of getting a lot of crops from the land. There are big advantages to intensive farming. It is one of the ways we have been able to feed the world's increasing population. And getting more crops from the same amount of land has helped to keep food prices low.

However, intensive farming also causes problems. One of them is that the farms use chemical fertilisers to help the plants grow. If a lot of fertiliser is used, the soil can lose its natural nutrients, and become acidic. This makes it harder to grow crops.

THIS IS NOT SUSTAINABLE!

For example, in Japan, the use of chemical fertilisers grew 300 per cent between 1950 and 1999.

1950
95 kg
per hectare

1999
290 kg
per hectare

This Japanese farmer grows her crops without using any chemicals at all.

BACK TO THE FUTURE

In some places, farmers are going back to techniques that were used before chemical fertilisers.

In Japan, almost all food is now grown using chemical fertilisers, but a small number of farmers will not use them. There is even a special name for crops that are grown without chemical fertilisers: *mukagaku hiyou*.

Some Japanese farmers are so determined not to harm the soil that they will not use ANY fertiliser. Even digging the soil or weeding are discouraged. This extreme form of sustainable farming is called *shizen noho*, which means 'natural farming'. *Shizen noho* crops are hard to find in the shops, but when available they are sold locally and in health-food stores.

BIODIVERSITY

Biodiversity is the name for the range of different plants and animals that live in an area. It is important to sustainable farming.

WHY IS BIODIVERSITY NEEDED?

Two of the main reasons are:

1) Today's crops are descended from wild plants. If wild plants disappear, it will be harder to find new crops in the future.

2) Some wild plants survive drought and pests better than ordinary crops. Using these as farm crops is a way for farmers to adapt to changing conditions.

BIODIVERSITY AND INTENSIVE FARMING

Intensive farming (see page 16) may harm an area's biodiversity. On intensive farms, chemicals are used to kill other plants, and insects that might damage the crop. The chemicals spread out and kill animals and plants nearby. This reduces biodiversity in the surrounding area.

At least 30,000 plants are edible

Humans only eat about 7,000 of them

There are 23,000 different plants around the world that could be used as food crops in the future.

Wild rooibos being picked in South Africa.

WILD TEA

Rooibos tea comes from South Africa. It is popular around the world, and is an important crop in its native country.

Rooibos only grows in a very small area of the country. Global warming is causing the climate there to get warmer and drier. The kind of rooibos farmers are currently growing may not be able to survive in the changing conditions.

Fortunately, a few people are still farming different kinds of wild rooibos. These are better at surviving in dry, hot conditions. In the future, they will mean the valuable rooibos tea industry can survive.

ORGANIC FOOD

People do not always mean the exact-same thing when they talk about organic food. But organic food usually has most or all of the characteristics listed below.

WHAT MAKES FOOD ORGANIC?

Organic food is usually:
- grown in a way that does not harm the environment
- produced without using chemicals, such as artificial fertilisers and pesticides
- not kept unnaturally fresh, for example by adding chemicals or using radiation
- sold close to where it has been grown

All these are things that help make farming sustainable. Eating organic food is not the ONLY way to eat sustainable food, but it is one way.

An Indian farmer throws unmeasured amounts of fertiliser over his crops. Using too much fertiliser quickly harms the soil.

Organic tea being picked.

THE SIKKIM ORGANIC MISSION

In 2003, the Indian state of Sikkim decided all its farms would become completely organic.

Sikkim's landscapes range from giant mountains to valleys with thick forests. There are many different plants and rare animals. The government wanted to protect this environment. Artificial fertilisers and pesticides were banned. Village by village, the government educated farmers about organic methods, and set up schools where people could study organic farming.

The policy has been a big success. Farmers are earning more, because they do not have to buy chemical fertilisers and pesticides. The natural landscape and biodiversity have been preserved. The government even says its people are happier than before they went organic!

MEAT AND VEGETABLES

Lots of people eat meat. Beefburgers might even be the world's most popular meal! And between 2010 and 2020, the amount of meat we eat is predicted to increase by 25 per cent.

MEATY PROBLEMS

The trouble is, meat uses more land and resources than any other kind of food. Beef (for those popular burgers) is the worst offender.

THE TROUBLE WITH BEEF:

Requires **160x** more land

and

produces **11x** more greenhouse gas ...

... COMPARED TO WHEAT OR RICE

COW BURPS

The world's cows are constantly burping out a gas called methane. Methane is one of the gases that is causing global warming. In fact, methane is 25 times as bad for the environment as CO_2.

Cow burps might not seem a big problem – until you realise there are almost a billion cows in the world. That's a lot of daily burps!

A tasty looking Veganuary (or any time of year) pizza.

VEGANUARY

Vegans are people who do not eat meat, fish or dairy products such as milk and cheese. Because it does not include meat or dairy, vegan food is very sustainable.

In 2014, a group of vegans in the UK launched 'Veganuary'. The name is a mash-up of 'vegan' and 'January', and the idea is that for the whole of January, people try a vegan diet.

Veganuary is a way for people to eat less meat, and see whether they like a vegan diet. The Veganuary website has hundreds of recipes and suggestions for meat-free food, to help people throughout the month.

THE SLIPPERY PROBLEM OF FISH

For about half the world's population, fish has always been the main source of protein. Proteins are needed for the human body to grow and repair itself.

As the world's population grew in the 1900s, so did the amount of fish caught each year. By the 1950s, huge 'super trawlers' were being used to haul in millions of tonnes of fish every year.

This amount of fishing was unsustainable. The numbers of cod plummeted. There were not enough young to replace the grown-up fish that had been caught. This made it almost impossible for stocks of fish to increase again.

1645–1750
8 million tonnes of cod is caught in 105 years

1953–1968
8 million tonnes of cod is caught in 15 years

COD FISHING ON THE GRAND BANKS

By 1994, cod numbers on the Grand Banks, off the coast of Newfoundland, had fallen by 99 per cent.

ICELANDIC COD

The Grand Banks cod fishing area is in the North Atlantic. There is a similar cod-fishing area near Iceland. The story of Icelandic cod fishing is very different from the Grand Banks.

Iceland's government is determined that its cod will not be over-fished. It sets limits on the number of fish that can be caught, and says that at least 20 per cent of the cod caught must be at least 4 years old, based on its size.

This is because four years is the age at which cod start to reproduce. If there are not enough cod reproducing, the ones that are caught will not be replaced by new fish. If this happens, the government reduces the amount of cod that can be caught in the following year.

A large Icelandic cod being packed. Fish this size are regularly caught in Iceland, but have almost disappeared in other parts of the North Atlantic.

FOOD AND WATER

Global warming is making droughts in farming areas more common. This is a big problem, because everything we eat needs water to grow.

WATER-HUNGRY FOODS

Of course, not all our foods need the same amounts of water to grow. Some use a lot more than others. Producing 1 kilogram of beef, for example, uses nearly 20 times as much water as producing 1 kg of apples.

Water-hungry foods are not sustainable. They drain the surrounding area, making droughts worse. The next year, there is even less water available for growing food. Eventually, the local water supplies dry out.

Growing 1 kg of apples uses 822 litres of water.

Growing 1 kg of wheat uses 1,830 litres of water.

Growing 1 kg of rice uses 2,500 litres of water.

Growing 1 kg of beef uses 15,400 litres of water.

Campaigners in New York City tell people the watery cost of eating beef: '1 steak = 50 baths'.

1 BIFE É IGUAL A 50 BANHOS peTA

CUTTING YOUR 'VIRTUAL WATER'

The water used to grow food is sometimes called 'virtual water'. In Europe, each person consumes enough virtual water to fill an Olympic swimming pool every 18 months.

Fortunately, being careful what you eat can reduce the amount of virtual water you use. The Water Footprint Network (www. waterfootprint.org) can help. Its website has an interactive tool called Product Gallery. Clicking on a food tells you how much water is used to make 1 kg of the food. For example:

• 1 kg of sugar from sugar beet uses 920 litres of water, but from sugar cane it uses 1,782 litres. It is best to use sugar from beet.

• 1 kg of potatoes uses 287 litres, but the same weight of rice uses 2,497 litres – almost 10 times as much!

WASTED FOOD

Imagine you are really hungry. Someone puts your favourite pizza in front of you. Then they cut the pizza into thirds, and take away one slice.

That slice represents how much of the world's food we waste every year.

ONE-THIRD WASTED

At least ONE-THIRD of the food we produce each year gets wasted. In poorer countries, food is often damaged during harvesting, or spoils in storage after harvest. In wealthy countries, a lot of food is thrown away because it does not look perfect. Also, fresh food is bought, then stored for so long at home that it spoils and has to be thrown away.

Wasting less is one simple, easy way to supply more people with enough to eat. Straight away, the world's food would become more sustainable.

One year's global food waste

=

Five years' food grown in Sub-Saharan Africa

Cassava being harvested in southern Africa.

THE US$1 MILLION CASSAVA PRIZE

Each year in Africa, enough food to feed 300 million people is wasted.

One of the staple foods in Africa is the cassava plant. Cassava grows underground, where it can last for a year or more and is able to survive droughts. But once cassava has been dug up, it starts to spoil within 15 minutes. A day or two later it has to be thrown away.

A charity called Yieldwise thinks the world's scientists can solve this problem. It has offered a prize of US$1 million to anyone who can come up with a way of keeping cassava fresh for longer.

GLOSSARY

compost rotted plants, added to soil to give it extra nutrients

dairy farm place where cows produce milk for sale

drought a long time without rain, which leads to a shortage of water

emission something released into the air, usually a polluting gas

fertile able to grow a lot of plants

fertiliser material added to soil to make plants grow better

fossil fuels coal, oil and natural gas, which are all fuels made from the ancient remains of plants and animals; burning fossil fuels releases CO_2

global warming increase in the Earth's average temperature

manure animal dung (poo) that is used to add nutrients to the soil

nutrient something that helps living things to grow and stay healthy

one-crop desert place where only one crop, and nothing else, grows

over-fish to reduce the number of fish disastrously by catching too many

pest an insect or other animal that attacks crops

pesticide a chemical used to kill creatures that could damage crops

plummet to go down very quickly

profit the difference between what something costs and what you sell it for

radiation invisible rays that can be used to kill the tiny organisms that make food go rotten

resources supplies of useful things, such as water or land

selling direct selling something straight to the person who will be using it

spoil to go rotten

staple most important

stocks reserves or stores of something

temperate not baking hot and not extremely cold; temperate climates are usually warm and sometimes damp

FINDING OUT MORE

WEBSITES

The Soil Association is a UK charity that sets rules about organic farming. You can find out more at: www.soilassociation.org

The supermarket chain Tesco has a special sustainability section on their website at: www.eathappyproject.com/schools-groups/ sustainability/in-store-trail

The Fairtrade Foundation website has information about the movement, and how to buy Fairtrade products: www.fairtrade.org.uk

The Marine Stewardship Council's website for children is a fun way to learn about sustainable fishing: https://fishandkids.msc.org/en

FURTHER READING

Food: From Field to Plate by Michael Bright
(Wayland, 2016)

How Did That Get In My Lunchbox?
by Chris Butterworth and Lucia Gaggiotti
(Candlewick Press, 2013)

INDEX